HEROES WITHOUT CAPES

For Robin,

poems by

Alice Osborn

Be your own hero – always!
in love + light~

Alice O

MAIN STREET RAG PUBLISHING COMPANY
CHARLOTTE, NORTH CAROLINA

Library of Congress Control Number: 2015948618

ISBN: 978-1-59948-539-3

Produced in the United States of America

Main Street Rag
PO Box 690100
Charlotte, NC 28227
www.MainStreetRag.com

Acknowledgments

The author wishes to thank the following editors, journals, and books where these poems, some in slightly different versions, first appeared:

When Women Waken: "Running with Snakes"
Broad River Review: "Cooper River Bridge," "My Parents' Wedding Day"
Referential Magazine: "Movies with My Father," "Meeting the Devil in Myrtle Beach outside Woody's, Hwy 17"
County Lines: "Midnight Meeting at the Crossroads near Clarksdale, Mississippi, circa 1936," "Dick's Ode," "Coffee Ode"
Poetry in Plain Sight: "Old Derelicts"
Comstock Review: "LBJ Takes Off"
Carolina Woman Magazine: "Ode to Hamburger Helper," "Southern Ice Storm," "Nolan, The Split Foyer, is Under Stress," "How to Remove a Carpet Stain"
Quantum Fairy Tales: "The Predator at the Super Walmart," "The Bear and the Maiden Fair," "The Sith Lord's Lament," "Boba Fett at the Chick-fil-A in Hickory, North Carolina," "I Slept with Boba Fett"
Flying South: "Entreaty to Young Editors"
Germ Magazine: "Dina, the Delta 70-Seat Jet"
Kakalak: "The Chorus Presents: Ripley of Acheron"
Pilcrow & Dagger: "Always on Sundays"

The author wishes to extend her gratitude to M. Scott Douglass, Richard Allen Taylor, Jane K. Andrews, Joseph Bathanti, Sara Claytor, and Boba Fett.

Introduction

Within this collection of dramatic monologues, odes and personal narrative poems, you'll meet some of the famous and infamous figures from history, myth and pop culture who show varying degrees of heroism. I picked them because their internal/external conflicts resonated with me or they inspired me when I was a kid. Some of these heroes are not "good" people, but they appear in my book because they have followed-through on their agenda. They didn't pander or skim—they did what they said they were going to do. Some of my heroes have killed before, as in the case of the hunters Predator and Boba Fett, but they have their own personal code of wrong and right. Some have made mistakes such as drinking too much, loving the wrong woman, racking up too much debt or allowing themselves to get in their own way. Many are in the middle of making a hard decision that will probably change their lives.

What makes a hero? A hero does the right thing when no one is looking; or they do the right thing never expecting any kind of reward. What makes a great character? She or he is likeable, tough and honorable. Or if someone is not a good person, they must own a cool cape and possess high intelligence. One of my favorite heroes is Will Kane (Gary Cooper) from the film *High Noon* (1952). Like in my poem, "Do Not Forsake Me, a Sonnet," Will, the town's retired marshal, has just married Amy Fowler (Grace Kelly) and is preparing to own a store in another state, but then comes the terrible news: the man he put away is coming on the noon train. Along with his three goons, they plan to terrorize the town and kill Will for vengeance. Will decides to stay, but no one in the town (not even his wife!) wants to help him take care of Frank Miller. The town believes if Will leaves, then their troubles will leave because Frank only holds a vendetta against the former marshal. This is the story about one man's decision to hold his ground when everyone else wants him to turn away. It is also a movie about death—one of my favorite themes. If Will doesn't face the killers he will die inside and will not fulfill his duties as a lawman—it doesn't matter that the townspeople don't deserve him—he has to stand up according to his personal code.

I teach the Hero's Journey in my memoir and fiction workshops. Starting with a death, the hero, who can be anyone, ventures from the known world to the unknown world. She is pursuing a goal and this goal can likely change before the hero gets what she wants. Along the journey the hero meets many obstacles, enemies, friends and a mentor. The hero experiences successes and then encounters a horrible failure, which I label the "Little Death," that takes place right before the climax. After the hero survives the Little Death and surmounts the climax, she returns to the "village" and is now able to teach and mentor within that community so that everyone is able to heal and thrive.

Any of my heroes in this book could be you. Have you been forced to make an unpopular decision? Have you done the right thing when no one is looking? Of course you have.

Heroes Without Capes may be about quirky characters from galaxies both near and far away, but they share the same vulnerabilities, fears and hopes that we do. Being a hero doesn't mean you're not scared; it means you push through the fear and do it anyway.

To all of my fellow writers and creatives on their Hero's Journey

Contents

Movies with My Father

I

We head in different directions at the video store:
he to the rack filled with girls popping out of their bikinis,
surrounded by men wrapped only in sheets;
and me to the sci-fi/fantasy section, hoping
for a long-awaited release of *Return of the Jedi*.
But no such luck. We meet in the middle
on the neutral green carpet
where I can't believe he wants both
Spring Break III and *Hot Girls XXX*.
"No, Dad, not those. They're stupid movies," I say.
He tells me to shut up. "I'm in charge here, not you."
He wins.

II

Dad takes me to the movies on Sunday summers,
and I pray there's no kissing scenes.
I'm sure the whole theater hears him
whisper, "Liplock, liplock!" Can the girl break away
from Captain Kirk or Superman or Indiana Jones?
No one smack lips again for the remaining
ninety minutes! I poke around in the popcorn tub,
feel the kernels sticking to my back teeth.

Running with Snakes

Sweat spreads like ink along my T-shirt
as my friend Bill runs slow.
We curb into the woods
behind the subdivisions,
watching for roots or snakes.

In May a black one skittered away
behind the bikes in my garage,
and a decade ago I hopped
over a yellow one seeking sunshine
while my son slept in his stroller.

Bill tells me he's repulsed by his wife
of 12 years. "I stay away from home nights."
Then he says, "I'm in love with someone else."

How do I judge distance, loss and time?
My own marriage is a snake—
mysterious and yearning for warmth,
sometimes we find heat again after months
of chasing kids, jobs and bills.
I often travel alone.

I nod in sympathy, and look down at a black root.
A slender six foot rat snake lounging in dappled heat.
Bill's impressed I didn't step on the reptile;
he doesn't know I don't make mistakes twice.

And then there's another on the path's carpet.
Copperhead or corn snake?

Ancient Chinese wisdom says meeting
a snake brings great luck.
What about luck squared?
Does the luck leave when you step where you shouldn't?

Bill demands I keep his secret,
coiled tight out of the sun.

Cooper River Bridge

Alongside thousands
of other bridge runners,
our bodies block the clear Charleston
sky and sea, as the eroding marshland
curls green beneath.

This pylon of silver,
its rivets like buttons on an old man's plaid shirt.
Billed birds cry to their companions,
scraping the brown muck of pluff mud
from their wings. That musty smell's
all in my drinking water,
algae compounds leaving spots on my wine glass.
They say refrigerate your tap water—
for a nice, clean taste.

Where would the Holy City
be without its liquid economic engine,
but also its brakes—high tides flood
downtown streets anytime it rains more than an inch.
Rain bombs overload the drainage systems.
And it's only going to get hotter.

I wipe sweat, adjust my hair clip.
A fellow runner in jean shorts and a dirty tank top praises,
"Thank you, Jesus!" as we lean our feet
into that first grueling hill,
built to accommodate container ships,
their holds grabbing nothing
but air and steel, port and prayer.

Meeting the Devil in Myrtle Beach
outside Woody's, Hwy 17

"Aren't I the one you're looking for?" he greeted me
at the restaurant door. I should have done laundry
or zoned out to VH1 instead of meeting friends for beers.
Who was this man with a bald head shaped like a squash,
a nimble slug in a Dick's T-shirt and jean shorts.

Who could be this fugly with such confidence?
I didn't mean to nod at, "Do you like dancing?"
He poked me with questions about lasagna. White or red?
He told me I preferred a bloody cardinal vintage.
"Karaoke?" He knew I sang every Wednesday night. Then
he asked me about any hoop piercings in my lady parts.

A smirk from his thick, swine lips. "You look like you have
a thick clit." How could he know or not know?
He smelled of Brut and Bensons & Hedges, not brimstone,
but, oh, yes, it was time to leave and take a different way home.

Damn my good manners.
Damn the concrete attached to my black mules.
Damn my shitty dating pool at this tourist trap.
Damn my heart's echoes.

I didn't mean to vaporize seven minutes from my life.
I didn't mean to never forget his face.

Midnight Meeting at the Crossroads Near Clarksdale, Mississippi, Circa 1936

I love the smell of burning trash, yeah, baby,
the smoke spreading out here at Highways 49 and 61.
Robert's right on time,
October moonshine
glints off his $25 guitar—
"Over here, Robert, let me tune it up for ya.
I hear you be bein' an okay harp player ain't enough."
Tonight I'm a big black man in my fifties,
but I can be any color, size or age. Even a woman.
That's how I appeared to Senor Paganini
before I gave him his gift.
Man, could he play the fiddle!
Only took them thirty-six years to find a resting place
for his long bones. No one rests after
we shake hands and I deliver.
Robert Johnson's another smart hobo,
aching for fame now,
not in a decade or two
when his knees fail and his fingers wither.
"Robert, let me play ya 'Cross Road Blues,'
my favorite." He hums, slaps his hand
to his thin side and grins, all white teeth,
while he licks out in the key of open A.
Then his fingers burn all over the neck, all them
sharps and flats he never knew before existed.
Our meeting takes ten minutes at most—
good, 'cause I still got to do a shitload of work tonight.
Thanks to me he'll be crowned
King of the Delta Blues,
but first he must be poisoned
and thresh to my whispers
in his dreams.

Old Derelicts

My wheels, scuffed and half-buried in the split
blanket of grass, circles of time repeating,
like my owner's circle on his left finger;
pale reminder of a lost commitment.

His cake-yellow hands no longer
grip my steering wheel
after parking me next to the barn
seven jobs, three states ago.

We built carports together in suburban D.C.
for one car, four-person families
where summer's humidity vacuumed choked air
and winter's glass iced cracked roads.

I remember him splicing wood,
sanding planks, a Winston between his teeth.
Tool belt slaps against the tailgate
as he fumbles fickle nails in my bed.

Imagine he creaks home to a singlewide trailer—
mildew traces the last rainfall along the siding,
and PBR cans form a Tic-Tac-Toe pattern
in the chain-link fence.

I stare ahead, sleep to the crickets
in the Chatham County twilight,
missing his voice, light like rain,
yet smoked with whiskey and dust.

LBJ Takes Off

Goddammit, all I want is a cigarette.
Everyone else is smoking,
what a sweat lodge, all shades closed up tight.
Boil at the back of my neck's gonna explode.
No one leaves Dallas till I say the word.
Our tents've been raided and our horses hobbled.

The morning team's out of office for good,
but hell if I'm the chief in the Irish mafia's mind.
So come on over, honey, get up from the bed,
I'm not about to stage a coup.
That's right, all the ladies 'round me,
Bird, Judge Sarah, sweet, sweet Jackie.

My hands don't shake, but hers do. Mercy.
They're bare, white—still lots of blood
on her pink outfit.
Don't see anything
but the flashbulbs. Thank God
for the smoke, or the scalp smell
she carries would kill us again.

"So help me God!"
I shout over the howling engines,
swearing on this stand-in Bible
Jackie snatched from the bedroom's nightstand.

Hatches shut tight,
the Colonel shoots us so hard
out of Love Field we're like
a Comanche's lance,
driving its steel point
into our surprised throat.

Dick's Ode

American Ajax, when the wise Odysseus
won Achilles's armor, instead of you,
you frothed to kill your own brothers,
who had slashed, stabbed and sweat rivers
at your shoulders.
When we needed a focused warrior
against al-Qaeda, you wiretapped,
waterboarded and detained.
How quickly they forgot you standing tall
against the lances and arrows,
shielding them once more
from the stockpiles and theocratic assassins.
Your borrowed heart
thumping for truth, justice and the Dark Side.
Tin Man from a tiny state
with no income tax,
you think apology is for the weak;
the ones who want to be liked.
Who cares if Harry Whittington meets Elysium
with thirty bits of birdshot.
But instead of going mad, killing sheep
and falling on Hector's sword,
you shrug off your flaws, like so many drops,
and would do it all over again today.

My Parents' Wedding Day

The ivory lace wedding suit is knee-length,
bought off the rack at Garfinkel's.
Professional, practical for a cold February day.
His arm touches the fur lining of her wrap,
they smile in mute tones before the cold ushers
them into a waiting Ford.

No photos of their wedding
ever lived in our house—
instead, my parents' single wedding photo,
the height of a coffee cup, rested in kind dust
on my paternal grandparents' mantel for thirty-five years.

What can explain my mother's aversion
to weddings? She barely attended
her own, on George Washington's birthday,
her day off, telling me at age five she married
to escape roommates. Or was it to fill in
for a dead father or get a Green Card?
She only invited one friend.
She forgot the exact date.

She has a knack
for being sick or staying home
with the dog on wedding days.
By my brother's second wedding
everyone expected she wouldn't show.
Ever the Catholic, she fears God will strike
with thousands of lightning darts
blazed in hot oil
for never loving her husband
of fifty years.

Do Not Forsake Me, a Sonnet

After our wedding I hung up my tin star,
while Frank Miller's men drank shots awaiting the noon train.
He's comin' for me from afar.
Dear Amy, wherever we go, they'll kill us out on the dusty plain,
so I turned the horses around. I didn't run.
The whole damn town, including you,
the judge, old friends are afraid of Frank's guns.
He's crazy and doesn't like to lose.
Maybe I'm a fool to act in this final show,
but he won't call me a coward.
Hear that train whistle's nasty blow,
it's high noon, Amy, don't be a doubter.
Stay with me, don't you leave.
Even when Frank takes my breath; you're all I need.

Captain Bligh: Adventures in Post Mutiny Rowing in a 23-Foot Long Boat

What the fuck, Christian?
Bloody fucking wanker.
You can't leave the King's Navy like you left
that whore yesterday with her brown hands
outstretched. No wonder you're fighting
off the clap—if you go back your pecker
will drop like a duck from a rifle shot.

*Row, men! Let's put some distance
between that traitor and us!*

I was probably too lax.
And you call *me* the pompous ass
when I kept everyone alive these past eighteen months.
I'm too demanding on the men?
Swabbing, press-ups and fiddle dancing?
Only whipped one man the whole voyage.
Bloody breadfruit trees. Bloody Tahiti.
Bloody paradise that erases
all sense of duty.
Bloody awful island women.
Never tasted those flowers
and I'm the healthier for it.

*It's going to be a glorious day!
How are we feeling, men?*

Now this is quite the situation. Fucking Sod's Law.
Christ almighty. I've got two dozen men to feed
with three days of rations and five days of water
in a fucking rowboat with a sextant and pocket watch.

You foreswear them, me and England.
Let's hope the natives are friendly—we have no muskets.
I will get my vengeance on you, Christian.
I will not die out here on this God-forsaken sea.

We've got 30 miles to Tofua—food, men.
All will be sorted out, you'll see!

This will not look good on my permanent record.
Ah, well, it could be raining.
Fuck. I left my hat in my cabin.

Benedict Arnold Sings the Blues

It's so easy to hate me,
we weren't supposed to win.
Cut the facts from fantasy,
weren't we all kin?
You may know me as Judas,
or the devil in a tricorn hat.
I never stopped surviving,
and died in a foreign land.

I'm a one-time hero,
who can't change the past.
I've done some bad, bad things,
and I won't take it back.

Books forget I led an army.
Eating candles, bark and a dog.
We danced with black snowy death;
I prayed every day to God.
Then the rumors started,
there'll be no statues in my name.
So I made West Point weak,
and I wouldn't play their fucking game.

Sold a country, sold my soul,
sold a lot for a little gold.
Had to pay my debts,
never felt free,
and I still can see my father
drowning in his whiskey.

Bruce the Shark

Never knew me father,
nor me mother, come to think of it.
Had to raise m'self and fight for seal pups
with my three brothers and sister.
We're swift predators out of Megatooth,
that haven't changed much in 28 million years.
Mum named me after Dad,
mad as a cut snake, died doing what he loved:
chomping surfers and sinking tinnies.
They don't forget what he did—
and now hunt us for soups, fertilizer and jewelry.
I grew a bit more and my 350 teeth came in.

Then, Marcia, Marcia! I smelled her a mile away
at Devil's Teeth. I got all show pony on her.
How could I not with her shiny denticles
and delicate snout. A week into our courting,
an orca drowned her and feasted.
I breached the surface many times,
the closest match for vengeance I could rip
into—pulping dolphins.

I was me father, a mindless killing machine.
Then I met Cal, a whale shark.
Very big, very laid back, very old;
only eating seaweed.
Told me a veggie diet could calm me down,
chill our image and render me a nice Brucey.
So I started a FF support group in Australia
for other meat-eaters. "Fish are friends, not food!"
I lit out for the Coral Sea.

Lordy, lordy, I still dream about seals
and the fun I had assailing them from below.
Their flesh soft like reef mangroves.
We meet every Tuesday 1:30 p.m. at the wall.
Chum the Mako coughs up a skeleton every now and then,
but Anchor relaxes with massages on his machine-tool head.
Can we beat evolution?
One fillet at a time, mate.

Call Me Stumpy

Never knew what hit me off Virginia Beach—
the bastard! I was going to be a mom
for the sixth time, a boy. Named him Jack,
after Jacksonville, Florida, where I mated
with … what's-his-name?
What lice spots! Such a gorgeous fluke!
Not broken and scarred like mine.
I met him near Grand Manan
on a foggy summer day. The Bay of Fundy
mating grounds. Something to do with those tides, I guess.
Last I heard he collided with fishing gear.
Three more of my mates died the same way.
The good scientists tagged and named
my family with a long string of numbers.
EG#1004. Don't know if the "E" stands
for endangered—that word puts me in a pickle.
A wrinkled, crinkled pickle.

Men call us right whales
because we're the "right" whales to hunt.
We float when we die so it's real easy
to catch our blubber and what not.
I was told Great Great Great Grandfather Klunkle
inspired Moby Dick, but wasn't he a sperm whale?
Big difference, you know. They have teeth
to eat up nasty ships and sailors.
Always wished I had teeth.
Anywhoo, can't help how we rights are
big black targets with barnacles.
I bet you could out swim me any day.

When I check on my bones
in the Raleigh museum,
Jack's still there in my belly.
Kids point and touch my ribs,
my messed up mandible …
my jaw got scanned and now the ships slow down.
I did something right! I made a funny!
Who cares if "what's his name" didn't like my jokes.

Less than four hundred of us left,
and me peacing out on the sunny first floor
dreaming of warm seas and crisp white krill.

Ode to Hamburger Helper

Come to me my enriched pasta and rice,
packaged cheese and red powdered sauce—
I pull out the milk and water for you
on school nights when the kids
are starving for Beef Pasta or Crunchy Taco.
My husband prays for your buck a box special at Food Lion,
a week of dinners—just kidding—but seriously,
I did you three times a week
when we were first married.

Well-meaning friends demand I open
a cookbook once in a while—
there's way too much salt
and MSG in your gloved Helping Hand boxes,
evoking a certain late pop star.
They tell me to avoid your yellow starches,
cook real pasta and veggies—forego the quick prep.
Run past Aisle 4—"Prepared Foods"—run!
And what the hell are you doing in Food Lion anyway?

They can keep their organic carrots and hand cut pasta;
I've got 27 Box Tops to collect for my son's school.
I blame my mother—oh, I know, but it's true!
She created all from scratch,
spent hours in the kitchen, and nary a Helper or a Kraft
noodle crossed my lips till I was twenty.
Like skirts, pendulums swing
and I love your Italian, Chicken and Asian Helpers
over browned lean beef.

I promise not to burn you.

The Predator at the Super Walmart

Beef! Need lots of beef!
Paper says Wednesday is day
for $2.99 a pound. After me eat beef
me watch *Sesame Street*. Yes!
Cookie Monster me favorite,
but all those cookies would mess up the insides.

Me pull up truck to open spot far away
from other vehicles—don't like people
parking too close and denting doors.
Last time find two new
dings. Me scream and scare shoppers.
Usual stuff. Wear helmet so don't
frighten people too much. Teeth do stick out a bit.
Don't buy bullets
or kill anyone at Walmart—just Target snobs.
Kidding. No one gets humor.

After shoving old plastic bags
into outside recycle bin, wipe cart down
with stinky wipes in tube. Cart
is too short, so use knuckles
to move it along. It's Wednesday, not Friday
when everyone buys movies, cigarettes and beer.
And guns. Me buy beef.

Ring butcher bell, and Charlie comes right away.
What wonderful service! And fills up cart.
Few ground chucks spill out and hit
feet. Ouch, me have tender feet like bananas.

Take cart to express line because
only one open. Me shouldn't, but clerk waves
me over anyway. Have more than ten beef packages.
Tattooed lady in short skirt behind me is mad.
"Get out of the express line, asshole!"
Repeat her words back at her.
Very loud. She keeps talking at me.
Imitating her fun!
How me learn to speak like you weak humans.
"Get in another line! You can't be in this one!"
She doesn't like her words in this mouth.
Her heat register now very high.
Pointing finger. Take off helmet.
She leaves quickly. Runs.
Out of store leaving
her Greek yogurt and tampons.
Clerk says sorry, and me want cookie.

How to Serve an Alien at Walmart

French toast and diesel—cloying and acidic.
I can smell him coming from Aisle 5.
Predator scares the shit out of me,
clomping in his gray boots through the produce section.
His scalps hit his armor in time to the stride.
Thank God he's wearing his helmet this time,
I've never seen him take it off,
but LaKesha at the front told me
he removed it last week when another customer
was rude to him. He could be banned for that.

Predator grunts, chirps and beeps like a Muppet.
Sometimes he mimics my voice.
Boy, that freaks me out. Maybe I can get him
to call up my girlfriend when I'm out playing poker.

After he rings my bell, I crane my neck up at his
seven feet. Maybe 300 pounds?
He's fit and can easily kill anyone,
but they have to be armed.
He has standards, you know.
Today he orders ground chuck 80 percent lean, beef tips,
eye round, shoulder round, skirt steak.
Never kabobs.
Okay, never anything else for that matter.
No veggies, cereal, milk, juice.
I think he did ask me once in a girl's voice
where he could get cigarettes.
A Lucky Strike unfiltered man.
Does he find our meat
moist and flavorful? Does he eat it raw?
Maybe put some A1 on it? Or use a fork?

Or tongs? A backhoe? Or does he even wait to get home?
Wonder what kind of car he drives? Ford 150,
    diesel I bet.
Does he make dinner for his girlfriend?
Guess I could ask, but nah…

"Thank you, Charlie."

His voice is scratchy like a far-off radio station.
Predator gently guides his cart to check out.
Whatever. He's our best customer.

Coffee Ode

Without you, Goddess Kaffeina,
as this nectar of creativity,
words drizzle on blank leaves
and the monkey mind checks Facebook
at the top and bottom of the minute.
Hours later, my purse leather retains your perfumed heat.
Stay the preventer of headaches and weak limbs
as I fight flash floods, picking up the kids
in a baby hurricane.

Just today I swallowed your fair trade cinnamon bean
ripened in shade-grown trees,
while writing longhand in my favorite café
with purple lamp shades
and yellow couches where thousands
of brewed drops have spilled.

Thanks to gulping your mocha ambrosia
while she expanded in my womb,
my six-year-old daughter steals sips
of my Sunday brew,
hooked for eternity
on condensing the mysteries
of a thousand-year-old berry
for the small price of water and electricity.

Southern Ice Storm

Freezing rain pinged the skylight
after the late news;
the Appalachians dammed
the air from New England.

Patti first hears the crack of the thin
Bradford pear branches,
then the boom of a collapsed
transformer. Then another. She tastes
the silent furnace hum.

The battery-operated radio says power
could return within the hour, but if not,
call someone. A cold banana and apple
must feed all four North Raleigh residents.

The minivan's engine runs
for twenty-five minutes,
the ice chunks mocking the contained
heat. Both parents chip and lift the frozen
sculpture to free wipers and headlights,
while inside
the eight- and three-year-old
overturn tables and etch suns
with Sharpies on the carpet.
"Do you have to go to work today?"
She already knows the answer.

At 7:12 a.m., his recall-free Toyota
attempts to escape their glassy driveway,
swaying and spinning like a drunk dinosaur
until the laws of friction engage.
For her, there's only home with no TV,
bored children and the crystal claws
knocking their unwelcome
against the wooden siding.

Nolan, the Split Foyer, Is Under Stress

Spawn of Satan!
Up and down house, fall risk.
Bad duct work, damp, moldy, effing ugly.
Come on, aluminum siding has its merits. Okay, had.
I'm a good house for the money,
try finding a better deal inside the Beltway.
I'll guarantee you exercise—
open the front door to six steps
to the kitchen and bedrooms,
and six to the rec room.
You can see everything from the front door,
good when it's a party, bad
when Grandpa is wearing his holey boxers.
I'm open, friendly,
just don't call me white trash with new paint.

They don't build my kind anymore;
everyone wants to live in a manor.
Good God, eight months on the market,
when will I get my new family?
The split levels, colonials, contemporaries, Tudors,
and cute little Dutch styles think they got it
going on with their cathedral ceilings,
kitchen islands, free-standing tubs.
I've got new beige carpets, a tile shower
and granite countertops in the kitchen.
But pregnant mom groans when she climbs
the stairs, worried about the baby falling.
Fat dad refuses to leave the foyer.
The five-year-old twins scamper
up and down twenty-five times,
hanging on my banister.
Gaze beyond my entry-way, why don't ya?

Between husbands and wives,
teenagers and parents,
mothers-in-law and daughters-in-law.
No divorces. No estrangements.
I've kept the peace for fifty-two years.
How about you?

How to Remove a Carpet Stain

The Big Dipper splotch
mocks me at the top of the stairs
guarding the bathroom, delighting in permanence.
Not coffee, tea or dirt.
Motor oil perhaps, but how the hell
did a member of my household
spill fuel from their hands or a plastic cup
before going to bed? Boiling water,
baby shampoo, toothbrush, prayer.
This stain is like a pole dancer
clinging to carpet fibers
before closing time.

I call the carpet guys
and they blame me for playing
Lady Macbeth. But in the wetness
of now scrubbed wall-to-wall,
the stain remains, a hero who
remembers that moment
of glory when strangers' thoughts
only centered on him
and now refuses to disappear.

The History of Paint

Drunk, my father
painted walls around the split level stairs
with White Dove OC-17.
Then he rolled a shiny gloss
into the rec room's brown paneling
to make it brighter and larger,
covering years of handprints, scratches,
kicks before we moved to other states.
What else does white hide?

Nothing was the same once inventors discovered
Charlton White, the first washable enamel,
conveniently available in tins for the man
of the house. Black marks
and sins erased thanks to the magic
of zinc oxide-based pigments.

Once I invited a date into my new apartment's kitchen,
handing him the merlot to open. He struggled
like a seal to open the cork, splashing
a pink polka dot cloud all over
the ceiling, fridge, laundry room door and floor.
I bought an Alabaster white for the occasion,
proud to cover up his mistake with a brush.
As if it were only that simple.

The Dutch revolutionized paint with oil,
the perfect binder using walnut extracts and lead oxide
to preserve wood from
weather, worms and wind. Never mind damage
to lungs and blood cells; the white lasted centuries.

My father doesn't paint his retirement house now—
all walls weakened by dog paws and cat scratches.
My mother doesn't want him to mess up again
or make the animals breathe in fumes.
I wonder if all he wants to do
is yank a brush, jam it
into the thick off-white paint
and roll-slap the acrylic until
only the tip of his nose remains pink.

Entreaty to Young Editors

Remember, folks, the delete key is your whacker
against acyrologia. You've killed a roach before, right?
Same thing.

Mr. Fornaciari, my sixth grade English teacher,
grew up poor in Boston and watched *I Love Lucy* re-runs
every day after school. When roaches crawled over his legs
he smooshed them with a tennis racket.
He said they smelled like apples gone bad.

Back in college and high on pot,
I flung a giant roach off my balcony
by making a toe claw with my right foot.

Years later while hosting an open mic
in downtown Raleigh,
Some in our audience jumped
like marionettes caught in turbulence.
Before the fat sucker could slink into a wall crack,
I killed him with the sign-up clipboard.

Compadres, to be a great editor,
lay waist all over the keyboard,
in your intimate and fare wisdom,
ring your fingers as the fumes
waif their decent and whale
like Lucy gobbling palates
of chocolate roaches
too sweet for her pallet.

Road Runner Has a Sex Change

I

When I was a chick in West Texas,
Mother left me alone in our den.
From the open door I studied our world:
green cacti with yellow flowers,
gauzy sun, blue nights, century plants
laced with dew in pink dawn.
I drew in my eyebrows, plumped my cheeks
and sang a song, "Meep Meep, I have big feet!"

II

A single mom,
she didn't have time to explain sex to me,
or else she was too embarrassed.
I always felt different:
too-long eyelashes, a skinny neck,
my Adam's apple bobbing like red berries in the breeze.
I liked boys, but couldn't tell anyone:
no flock pariah situation for me.
I saved my secret, practiced running,
my size 13 feet carrying us
to #1 Desert High Cross Country Champs, 1947.

III

I had a few dates with girls, a peck on the beak,
then I raced home to cry into my teddy bear.
I had dreams of running away
to California where I could
find a good doctor to make me whole.

IV

At the initiation ceremony for full birdship,
my friends and family said a few words:
"Jimmy will achieve great heights."
The usual rhetoric, blah blah.
I packed my toothbrush, washcloth,
pack and transistor radio, left early the next day.
California, watch out!

V

Then I met my stalker in Carson City, Nevada.
A young coyote by the name
of Wile E. (E for Ethelbert I later found out).
He cut me off on the canyon road and I shouted,
"Meep Meep, *Dogius Ignoramius*!"
while flicking my tongue at his brutish muzzle.
He decided *I'd* make a good meal.
The game was on—I got waylaid
for thirty years.

VI

I worried for Sisyphus when he didn't rise
from his chalk line.
His Acme explosives didn't listen to their master.
I felt a little love for the old dog—
but tomorrow I have an appointment
three hundred miles away.
Cash sprinkled down on me from endorsements:
Plymouth, the state of New Mexico,
Time Warner and Honey Nut Cheerios.
Skirts won't look funny on me anymore.

VII

I sit in this office waiting for the surgeon,
yellow beak buried in a magazine on how
to get a man to notice me.
The first thing I'll do after we're done
is buy extended lash mascara in lush black.

The Lesbians Next Door

I wondered if being gay was contagious,
if my parents would stop loving me
if I liked girls. I remember Dad
saying, "It's good to have two kids,
just in case one is gay."

After the three women moved
into the raised ranch next door
they only allowed women to work on their house:
female plumbers, carpenters, roofers.

Mom quickly sized up the roommates
before they unpacked their boxes.
She told me not to talk to them,
or to their yellow dog with a different
name every Thursday. Mom and Dad
imagined their wild sex life
and I'd shut my ears when I'd catch
on their lips,
Daughters of Sappho, the Isle of Lesbos, lesbian.

One drove a Jeep and worked for UPS,
another sunbathed in her orange bikini
every Saturday afternoon,
and the fat one supplied groceries.
All had short hair.

Some night, I spied their big party
on their gray concrete patio from my side window.
My former PE teacher even came. The women
walked in and out of the sliding glass door,
beers in their hands nodding

to the Pointer Sisters' "Jump for My Love"
and "I'm So Excited."
They hugged and kissed.
I stood on my twin bed,
head tucked like a turtle
under my white roll-up shade,
eyelashes to the glass.
I wondered why the fat one
told them to all come in,
later realizing the streetlight cast a silhouette
of my ten-year-old head.

Dina, the Delta 70-Seat Jet

How many times a day do I have to see your butt crack
when you jam your bags in my overhead bins?
Why so much cleavage at 9 a.m.? Lordy mercy!
So many pet peeves, so little time.
People used to dress up to fly—not anymore.
Cream-colored ladies' suits from Bloomingdales, hats, gloves.
Women wore slips back then. You could taste the class!
Oh, holiday travel is the worst. Six weeks
of kids peeing on my seats, spitting up Cheerios.
My plumbing needs a good shakedown
and what's that irritating squeak coming from my brakes?
My wings need patching!
Where's my cleaning crew? Budget cuts.

Why wasn't I asked to host *You're Wearing THAT?*
I remember Jackie before Jack was an airport folks try to avoid.
You can be totally "come hither" with a high necked sheath
and long necklace. Or wear a cute belt and high heels.
Keep the hemline at the knee or slightly above and wear
any color but black. However, if you do wear black, wear
a bright-colored belt to look less funereal.
The biggest pet peeve of mine is if it's too tight,
go up a size or get you some Spanx.
If your clothing's too loose, get you to a good tailor shop.
For the guys, don't get me started on pleated Dockers,
white socks with dark shoes or socks with sandals.
Shoes should be shined, or at least cleaned up.
And socks can't have heel holes—I can't imagine the state
of your Tighty Whities.

Ouch, another controlled crash at LaGuardia,
please… I need a fog delay—some rest!
I need time for all of the fashion mags left on the seats.
I'm not an heir to fashion, but an heir to sense.
My mother inspired modesty in me, among other things—
but I won't get into that because that's a whole 'nother workshop.

What Really Happened to Mary

Greetings, my child! I am Gabriel, the Lord's messenger.
Do not be afraid.

> Wow, what big golden wings you have!
> You smell like almonds—okay, now I'm hungry.
> I thought you saw only kings and priests.
> Do you bring good tidings—will Joseph finally set a wedding
>   date?

Ah, no. So highly favored, the Lord is with you.
Tonight you shall conceive the Lord's child in your womb and name
*   him Jesus.*

> What?!? Are you kidding me? That's crazy, mister!
> I can't have a baby now. I'm a virgin.
> Believe me, Sir Angel, we almost did it two days ago,
> but I said no. Joseph will think I've cheated on him. He'll stone me.
> Oh, why me?

Blessed are you among women. You've been expressly selected.
We all trust you to have faith, like your cousin Elisabeth
who is with child. The Lord's doing, of course.

> Elisabeth is pregnant? No way. She's so old.

Mary, it's true. God is very handy with fertility
in old and new wombs. He's been watching you
your whole life and knows you will be a superb mother to his child.
A child who will make the world a more peaceful place.
You're our Chosen One. But it must be tonight.

Tonight, huh? I'm honored by the invitation,
but nothing will be the same again.
You're making my life hard!

Mary, do you want to be ordinary and average?
Don't you want to be noticed for your faith? Inspire others?
Your ancestors will be very proud of you. Mother to the son of God!

Yeah, easy for you to say—I've got to live with
all the surly comments—so will Joseph if he still
wants me. But he is righteous.
Okay, fine. I'm up for the challenge.
Tell God I'm ready to let some love in.
But I want some respect. From now on
please refer to me as "The Virgin Mary."
Need to restore the gravitas and such.

As you wish. Now lie back, relax and let the Holy Spirit wash over you.

Hail Mary!

August 31, 1997

Thanks to the front page,
I found out like most people:
how she lay dying in a Paris tunnel,
how the impact raked her in like soft hay in a baler.
With Binky the Siamese cat plopped on my lap,
I stopped spreading strawberry jam on rye toast,
his skin folds and dusty white fur escaping over the print.
I wished he could lick all of that black type and spit up
a vicious hairball I'd shovel inside wet beach sand.

Loss reminds you about change,
and what you are willing to throw away.

One week later it's too early
for the calls of pelicans and egrets,
as I drive to a friend's home on Folly Beach
to view the prince-demanded funeral. I could
have watched at home, but her day demanded witnesses.

My boyfriend didn't know who she was
and couldn't understand her power.

It's the second time in eighteen years
I've set my alarm to see such pageantry.
Eight horses carry the hearse
instead of the bridal carriage.
I cry more for her than I did
for any family death. I cry
for another death coming.

It's time for me to move out of his place,
tell him what he's afraid to say,
and take his fat cat and a few towels in the parting.

The Chorus Presents: Ripley of Acheron

Against our constant warnings,
You have five minutes to evacuate!
she descends in the elevator,
shedding her blue jacket, shedding her mind-killers—
always watchful with her duct-taped
pulse rifle and flame thrower to rescue
the girl, her Persephone from
the Queen of the Eggs.
This Demeter is something of an immortal—
while in cryo-sleep she outlived her Earth daughter
and once returned to her planet, chose
a space station's safe orbit, refusing
to walk barefoot in the prairie grass
or view stars burning with death.

She brings her own star justice to the Queen's eggs,
dripping with mucous as one hatches…
saving the girl before the pomegranates eat her.
Angels hum to the sulfured air.
The two rise to the unstable surface,
what was rage in her descent is now fear.
You have two minutes to evacuate!
This wounded goddess could lose everything;
she's fighting gods with their own agendas—
before it was only her and her vengeance.
You have thirty seconds to evacuate!
The android Hermes flies
to mother and daughter before enfolding them
aboard the *Sulaco* as the dead world explodes.
The humans and near human flinch
to shock waves rising higher and higher
in the moon's atmosphere.

But all we know Hades won't let
Persephone ever leave
the underworld.

The Bear and the Maiden Fair

"What do you pray for, Ser Jorah?"
she once asked.
"Home," I replied.

Today I cross the borderlands with this girl,
the Khaleesi, no more than seventeen summers.
Three days ago she lost her son.
Two days ago she lost her husband.
Yesterday, she nursed three dragons,
the last wild things I saw in this red waste
that sprawls into heartbreaking infinity.
Without water the horses will die
in two days and so will we.
What vision for us does she see in her dreams?

She didn't notice me watching
her tuck a dirty strand of her blond hair out of her eye,
nor eat the peach I gave her from our stop in the oasis,
nor rub her chapped lips together.

Here in this savage land the people have no words
for "Thank you" but a hundred for horses.
My fair wife Lynesse hated the North
and left me for summer and a man without a beard.
Now I can't remember her face
nor what she liked best for supper.

I will always be your devoted knight:
a former slaver with bad knees, bad debt and a bald spot.
A traitor. I spied on you in exchange for a royal pardon,
to return to Bear Island,
but that was before you made me your pilgrim.

I Am Boba Fett, the Most Notorious
Bounty Hunter in the Galaxy

Sliding through the Sarlacc monster,
I landed on this planet without real space travel.
A primitive place where the natives
eat crawfish donuts and drink sour black coffee.
New Orleans. Found my way to bail enforcement school,
graduated top of my class.
I was living in the American Can
when Katrina hit. Thugs attacked,
making the scum at Jabba's Palace seem civil.
No one stole our boat. My new buddy Big John
got his 255 people off the building.
Every minute I brought down hard justice
with any weapon that fired—
the universal plea is, "Wait, wait,"
before their eyes blink and bodies brace.

Lost like a dog, I followed Amy to Asheville.
Smart and well-read, but she didn't pay her car loan—
her Prius got towed while she was sleeping in it.
Can't date a woman so irresponsible,
plus she looked like shit on account
of living in her vehicle.
Told me I'm emotionally unavailable
and a drunk. Can't argue with that.
Called up the same folks who towed Amy's car,
doing repo now before I'll get back into hunting.
A stare's all it takes before my targets
hand over their Corvette keys.
"Wait, wait."
Still the best damn thing I hear.

What Katrina Taught Boba Fett

for John Keller

No matter how many dogs we fed, they kept dying.

Get the white people on the roof of your building if you want
    water and food dropped.

I'm a terrible swimmer, but I couldn't let Big John down, so we
    made it a competition who could loot the Winn-Dixie first
    for charcoal and vodka.

Old people and pigs float the same way.

Don't cross Big John after he promised an old woman her oxygen,
    a man his heart medication, and a pregnant woman a safe delivery;
    he killed more deserving gold teeth and medallions
    than I can ever account for.

You know you're fucked when the police tell you, "Good luck,"
    and hand you their boat keys and uniform jackets.

Beautiful ugly New Orleans where I danced to jazz drums and found
    an unholy love for pork butts won't be my home anymore.

An eighty-two-year-old lady called me her hero.

The Sith Lord's Lament

Destiny lied.
We had them in our grasp. Everything was perfect. Planned.
Rebels. I underestimated them.
Who could have fixed the *Millennium Falcon* that fast?
No chance she could make the jump
with a deactivated hyperdrive.
How could the same titanium screws
that sustain my arms, legs, lungs
cost me my son?
We are the pawns of our parts.

I didn't alter the fate of the galaxy today.
Captain Solo survived, Fett earned his pay—
seven hells, is that psycho the galaxy's only competent hunter?
He disintegrated Luke's family, my family.
Oh, and his absolute insolence about his beloved bounty!
But we go back decades—he knows far too much about me.

Let me sip a fine Alderaanian ale;
if I could smell or taste the rich cherries,
not this metal for twenty-two years.
Need to seem angry and pensive on deck. Pacing is good.
Pacing looks like I've got a plan.
I am a great black bird
with terrible wings. Breathe.

I can't remember my love's face anymore,
only her soft voice and skin like honey.
Padmé would be proud of our son and hate me all the same.
How many have I killed over the years? Mother, do you forgive me?
I gave them all quick deaths. For you, always you.
I wish the same mercy for myself.
I'm certain Fett showed Owen and Beru mercy.

Admiral Piett holds his throat,
afraid I'm going to Force-choke him
and smash his breadstick body into the bridge shield.
What a smarmy sycophant, but he is creative.
I think I'll keep him.

Why couldn't Luke give in to the Dark Side?
Found and lost in twenty minutes.
After he escaped the carbon freeze,
I had to show my cards,
had to cut off his sword hand.
What kind of nut jumps down a reactor core?
I am a complete disappointment.
How can I overthrow the Emperor now?
That son of a bitch can read
all of my thoughts and is always two light jumps ahead of me.
He's going to birth a Bantha. No, make that three Banthas.
Yes, I'll tell him I went completely over budget
on the Skywalker retrieval mission. I'll just redouble my efforts
and crush the Rebellion in a few swift strokes.

Blast. I hear the tap of Piett's boots.

"Lord Vader, the Emperor is on Line 1."

Let's Make a Deal

Predicatable. Instead of relaxing with spiced rum and a good book,
I walk into my room finding Princess Leia Organa chained to my
bedpost. The guards keep thinking I'm this sexual gundark; but
they'll all lose their bets. I won't bow down to Jabba's sick games.
She's doing some weird breathing technique. Puffing up her cheeks,
hissing out air like a cat. Organa looks a lot younger up close.
And more crazy than the last time we met on Cloud City. And
ravishing. I take out all of the power cells from my rifles, place
them in the safe and then unchain her neck and small wrists. I don't
underestimate her, but there's more than one way to subdue. And I
don't waste opportunity nor fate. The timing's right.

   What do you plan to do with me, Fett?

Nothing. But everyone else here wants to fuck you. I believe it's
immoral to have sex before marriage. But you should hang out with
better men than Solo.

   What—like you?

Drop and run, drop and run—been Solo's MO for years. But I'm
happy for you both—tells me a lot about you and who you like to
hang out with.

   You don't know shit about me.

More than you think. There's more class in your thumb than in
Solo's whole soul or the souls of his spectral ancestors. Anyway,
here, have some of my rum and you're probably hungry. And cold.
I've got some fresh rations here somewhere…Jabba forgets to feed
and water his slaves, and leaves it to me to make sure no one passes
out. I've got a spare cloak…

Oh, this is good. You think you can get me out of here?

Hmmm…I could buy you from Jabba in the morning. Very big "could." Don't know if I can afford so much trouble. Then release you at Mos Eisley. Isn't Skywalker going to rescue you?

Nonsense—no one's coming. I failed. But you could help us.
Join the Rebellion—

You've got 20,000 credits in that bikini? The Rebellion doesn't pay shit. But maybe we could work out a deal.

I thought you said you don't want sex.

You do have a dirty mind. I like that. No, I think we can both help each other. I was going to use Skywalker, but you're smarter. I want to topple your father.

What good would that do? My father's dead.

Not your adoptive father, Princess. Your real one. We go back over twenty years. I even knew him when he was a Jedi. He pays well and on time, I'll say that. I'd have him killed already, but who wants the Empire forever on their ass?

Are you saying…Darth Vader? My father? The man who blew up my planet? Stop mind-fucking with me!

You know the real truth. Somebody just had to tell you straight. Vader doesn't know you're his kid. Or maybe he does deep down. Remember in the carbon-freezing chamber I tried to shoot the Wookiee? Vader stopped me. Probably because without the

beast you'd have no protection. Hmmm…but he really wanted
Skywalker. His boy. You must block him from sensing who you
really are. You're Skywalker's twin. So obvious it's scary and Lord
Asshole doesn't even know with his Force powers.

>   *Stop it. You're scaring me. Vader's my father—Luke's my brother?*
>   *How do you know all this shit?*

Ben Kenobi told me years ago—that was the deal for his protection.
Today I'm cashing in.

>   *Obi-wan betrayed us—what a little bitch! Good thing he's dead*
>   *already. Why didn't Luke tell me about Vader? But that's why he*
>   *kept mumbling, "Father, father" for days. Oh, shit—I kissed him.*

Sorry, honey, it's a lot to digest. You've got to consider these things
before you breed with Solo. There's some crazy genes. Maybe you
and Vader can save the galaxy together—end the war. Kill the
Emperor. But then that would affect my bottom line. Good thing
I've got a flush retirement account in a very secure location.

>   *Why tell me, Fett?*

Three reasons: one, you're not stuck up anymore thinking you're
better than me. Two, Vader is an asshole and I want him brought
down. Get him to surrender. He's strong-arming my people for
our wheat. They're starving. I didn't used to care, but…after it's
over you're going to be our ambassador and serve the Mand'alor.
Forever. You're our last hope, unfortunately. Three, I lost my father
as a boy. Yours is still alive. Maybe he's not the daddy you want, or
any of us wants, but if he's breathing, there's hope. And there's a
fourth reason I'm not proud of: I heard you like bad boys.

*You sure have a lot of faith in me, Fett. I agree to your terms after
you buy me from Jabba and I'm safe. Now take your helmet off.*

Not if you're going to slap me, thank you.

*You've been more open and honest with me than anyone I know. I
want to see your face. Your eyes. I bet you have scars on your
forehead…*

I comply and drop my helmet onto the bed. Her mouth is open,
ready. She moves in close for a peck on the cheek, but then she
kisses me on the lips with such force my neck almost snaps off.
Organa strips off her slave dress, fumbles at my codpiece, while I
bite her tongue until I taste blood. Screw celibacy. I should throw
her in the 'fresher and lock the door from the outside, safe from her
screams. I should don my earplugs, pick up my book and take a sip
of rum, but instead I singlehandedly fuck up the fate of the galaxy.

I Slept with Boba Fett

He's snoring; a light gasp.
Soon it'll be morning
and we'll be back in our masks.
My leg kicked his during my nightmare.
The old one where someone in charge tells me
I'm wrong and I'll die for it.
He reached out to rub my knee,
his touch soft like feathers.
Who's black or white in this world?
He's dangerous. So am I.
All these labels; I've killed too.
I'm sleeping with a gray man
who relies on wits and weapons.
This plan to ally with Fett
to save my friends is ultimately selfish.
And it will never happen.
Gray man meet gray woman.
I can't run fast enough
over the line I just leapt over.

What's up with this pile of real books
all around the bed?
I peg him as a psychological horror fan,
especially after he told me
who my father is. I'm too scared
to face Vader—what if he turns me
to the Dark Side? I'm so close to it.

I still love Han Solo, but something broke
out of me during the six months I stalked Fett—
memorized the strange symbols on his light green armor,
studied the tilt of his bucketed head,
learned his native tongue, imagined piloting
Slave I with him through black holes and quasars
with a reliable hyperdrive;
deeply jealous of the freedom and wealth
he collects in his canvas pouches.
The richest man in the galaxy owns one suit.

How do you sleep with someone?
Stay close or spread out?
I wish someone had told me.
How do you sleep with the man
who sold Han to the highest bidder—twice?
Six months ago my mind scrolled
through twenty scenarios
of how we would meet—I'd hit his jaw
and then his hunter's hands would guide down my hips,
while his lips slipped in mine.
Those same hands cradle the rifle
he holds like a newborn. I want
to cook him breakfast; scrambled eggs in red spice.
No. His palate probably prefers rations,
nothing too sweet or spicy.
I want him to burn through me again,
painting his salt on my legs, belly and back.

"Leia…wait, wait."

Boba must be caught in a bad dream,
so it's my turn to kiss his shoulder;
hover and hold until his muscles go limp.

He'll always be my scar that won't fade
when I'm back in the real world.

Boba Fett Escapes the Sarlacc Monster

for Rust Cohle

What the hell?
Two seconds ago my wrist shooters killed
three of Jabba's guards, wounded a fourth,
but Solo stopped my private mutiny with a staff,
activating my jet pack, hurling me down
the Sarlacc's throat—a vagina with teeth.
Looks like this bitch gets the last laugh.

Jabba didn't agree to sell me Leia,
even though I offered to waive his next fee.
Then things got even better.
After Skywalker killed the Rancor, Jabba
voluntold me to work security on his Sail Barge
to make sure Leia's friends walk the plank
so Ms. Sarlacc can digest them for a thousand years.

Coping, I drank a few spiced rums at the bar.
When the Jedi zapped open his lightsaber,
no one could tell I shot at my own side.
Before I could unchain Leia, I flew headfirst into the pit.
So here I am in a stomach chamber,
full of acidic spores, smelling of sour milk.
Will my armor keep me from breaking like a cracker?
Good-bye cape, scalps, antennae.

My friend Rust once said when he killed,
he imagined his marks welcomed it—
they let go of their hate, love, memories and pain.
Death turned into a dream with a monster at the end.

I don't want to let go or maybe I do.
Then I fall—dying's not so bad,
it's the waiting part. Please, let me pass out.
Maybe Leia and all of them got away;
she slept with me first. She chose me.

Sometime later, I'm thrown into the smell of fresh cut grass—
it's so hot and humid. Am I dead? No, I've got to pee.
Armor still on, but no helmet.

Rust also told me time is flat,
like a stacked spinning spiral of nebulas.
We do the same damn
mistakes over and over again.
Man, could I use a drink right now.

Boba Fett in AA

Barely nine, my father gave me
a miner's helmet to see in the dark—
we explored a deep cave
on the other side of our water world.
No light to the sides, only in front.
My arms trembled. Hard. Father noticed
and said he gets scared too,
but Fetts don't quit.
His voice guided me to bend my body, extend
one hand, then another glove to the damp walls,
smelling the snails and rot.
He begged me to push up like a blind fish
out of a seaweed tangle
to the circle in the cavern, my headlight mixing
with Kamino's moon.

I hear him say, *Keep moving,* in this cold room,
where we clutch our Styrofoam coffees,
where I can't hide behind my helmet,
the same one he wore before he lost his head.
Father's words sustained me as I almost
drowned in the Sarlacc's acids,
and somehow got shoved out to this world.
I'm free to change my story:
no Jedi, no Han Solo, no Leia.
When will I forget that woman?
But disintegrating into wine and whiskey won't help.

Dear God, grant the serenity to accept
the things I cannot change.

"Hi, Bubba."
Most Southern humans can't get my fucking name right.
Can't let it bother me now.
After all, I never took shit from Vader.

Boba Fett at the Chick-fil-A
in Hickory, North Carolina

My spent leg drags over the brown tile,
as graceful as a Bantha.
Sure, the Mandalorian body armor holds
my knee together, but I'm getting too old for this shit.
Tired of the nights camped out in my truck,
waiting for skips to duck out.
Tired of combing through databases till 3 a.m.
looking up license plates.
Tired of dressing up as a UPS dude
to gain access into their double-wides.
Eating nothing but Snickers for three days.

"Your Number 2, please.
A tall Coke. No ice. To go. Thanks."

I hit the head
and run into Jeremiah 29:11 in bold print:

For I know the plans I have for you,
plans to prosper you and not to harm you,
plans to give you hope and a future.

It's laughable like AA meeting coffee,
the garish rabbits and rainbows,
but I can't unsee it.
Recovery has taught me to accept the things I cannot change,
like my father's murder or losing Leia to Han Solo.
Hardship is the pathway to peace, they say.
Doling out violence and fear are my defaults
and my sponsor knows I still can't surrender to anyone.
Perhaps I need new expectations.

Holding the door for an old man in a Braves hat,
I keep my eye out for movement among the parking lot pines,
and mutter a tiny prayer while backing out by the drive-thru.
Then an even bigger one when I take a bite
before heading east to Raleigh.
I tell myself this ketchup on my armor is real,
even if the past isn't.

Boba Fett Tries Some Networking

The sign-in lady watches me scribble
my first name with a Sharpie, stick the tag on my polo,
and grab the red drink ticket.
Water will do fine—bars, cantinas—no difference.
Look at that creature guzzling his last drop,
yeah, that was me a month ago on a cracked cushioned stool.
Finally shaved off the beard and mullet—
no need to render myself invisible when the shit goes down.
No more scanning the wine aisle at the Cameron Village Harris Teeter
cradling my bottle with both hands,
afraid someone will take it.

Don't know anyone here in this crowd of 300,
but that tall guy in the black jacket
is trying to pick up the blonde Realtor
judging from her earnest smile and dangling earrings.
Lots of hot women arriving after their salon vists,
fanning their business cards,
flicking their purses when they decide time's up.
When they ask what I do I say, "Headhunter,"
hand them my new cards with my LinkedIn address.

The chatter bounces off the walls—poor insulation,
I see no fire alarms—OCD is kicking in.
My throat aches even though I haven't said anything.
Lapping the room twice, I inhale a barbecue sandwich—
the vinegar kills me. I miss a sweet mustard base.

She's not here. And I cannot change that.
We lost each other a long time ago.
Although that married redhead
smooths down her jacket and plants her elbows
on her non-existent hips like Leia.

"What do you do?" I say after approaching Red and her circle.
Start with a question—show interest; this is how you make friends.
She's a lawyer wanting to partner with someone like me—
reliable and no disintegrations.
But Red's hand stays on my arm too long,
and her voice sears like clean whiskey.
Not again. And she's got a big ring.
I excuse myself, picking up another sandwich to go.
But I turn around and push back through the oak door:
I'm tired of getting all my new business from strangers.

Always on Sundays

Next to the Safeway
where Dad got his *Washington Times*,
we cased the doors of the Church of Marvel,
aka Joe's Books.
No speaking allowed in the dusty sanctuary
where the congregation gathered
by the racks of fresh comics out every Wednesday.
While in the back,
next to the "Sacks are Loaded" baseball card trading dude,
my father ingested new history tomes
dumped off by a World War II widow.

Joe oversaw the service
from behind a wooden podium, no inkling
all comic book men hereafter will clone
themselves after his chubby belly, beard
and supreme fondness for faded KISS T-shirts.
Every week I searched for *Star Wars* #65
in the back issue bins with Leia and her blaster—
the one Dad ripped up in front of me
when he was drunk. Never found it.
While cleaning the register glass,
Mrs. Joe yelled at me if my index finger
lightly turned the cover's lower right hand corner,
just like my dad taught me—
who wants to buy a sucky book?
I felt so shamed
in her limp ponytailed presence,
but I deeply prayed to this kind of religion.